Published by Angelis Publications
ISBN: 978-1-912484-08-9
Cover Design Angie J Anderson

When you work, then really work. And when you play, really play! When you work, then really work. And when you play, really play! When you work, then really work. And when you play, really play!

Welcome!

Date / Name / From	Comments

Date / Name / From	Comments

Date / Name / From	Comments

Date / Name / From	Comments

Date / Name / From	Comments

Date / Name / From	Comments

Date / Name / From	Comments

Date / Name / From	Comments

Date / Name / From	Comments

Date / Name / From	Comments

Date / Name / From	Comments

Date / Name / From	Comments

Date / Name / From	Comments

Date / Name / From	Comments

Date / Name / From	Comments

Date / Name / From	Comments

Date / Name / From	Comments

Date / Name / From	Comments

Date / Name / From

Comments

Date / Name / From	Comments

Date / Name / From	Comments

Date / Name / From	Comments

Date / Name / From	Comments

Date / Name / From	Comments

Date / Name / From	Comments

Date / Name / From	Comments

Date / Name / From	Comments

Date / Name / From	Comments

Date / Name / From	Comments

Date / Name / From	Comments

Date / Name / From	Comments

Date / Name / From	Comments

Date / Name / From	Comments

Date / Name / From

Comments

Date / Name / From	Comments

Date / Name / From	Comments

Date / Name / From	Comments

Date / Name / From	Comments

Date / Name / From	Comments

Date / Name / From	Comments

Date / Name / From	Comments

Date / Name / From

Comments

Date / Name / From	Comments

Date / Name / From	Comments

Date / Name / From	Comments

Date / Name / From	Comments

Date / Name / From	Comments

Date / Name / From	Comments

Date / Name / From	Comments

Date / Name / From	Comments

Date / Name / From	Comments

Date / Name / From	Comments

Date / Name / From	Comments

Date / Name / From	Comments

Date / Name / From	Comments

Date / Name / From

Comments

Date / Name / From	Comments

Date / Name / From	Comments

Date / Name / From	Comments

Date / Name / From	Comments

Date / Name / From	Comments

Date / Name / From	Comments

Date / Name / From

Comments

Date / Name / From	Comments

Date / Name / From	Comments

Date / Name / From	Comments

Date / Name / From	Comments

Date / Name / From	Comments

Date / Name / From	Comments

Date / Name / From	Comments

Date / Name / From	Comments

Date / Name / From	Comments

Date / Name / From	Comments

Date / Name / From	Comments

Date / Name / From

Comments

Date / Name / From	Comments

Date / Name / From	Comments

Date / Name / From	Comments

Date / Name / From	Comments

Date / Name / From	Comments

Date / Name / From	Comments

Date / Name / From	Comments

Date / Name / From	Comments

Date / Name / From	Comments

Date / Name / From	Comments

Date / Name / From	Comments

Date / Name / From	Comments

Date / Name / From	Comments

Date / Name / From	Comments

Date / Name / From	Comments

Date / Name / From	Comments

Date / Name / From	Comments

Date / Name / From	Comments

Date / Name / From

Comments

Date / Name / From	Comments

Date / Name / From	Comments

www.ingramcontent.com/pod-product-compliance
Lightning Source LLC
Chambersburg PA
CBHW080811020826
48982CB00017B/860

* 9 7 8 1 9 1 2 4 8 4 0 8 9 *